Need to Know

Body Piercing
and Tattooing

Paul Mason

Heinemann
LIBRARY

www.heinemann.co.uk/library

Visit our website to find out more information about **Heinemann Library** books.

To order:

 Phone 44 (0) 1865 888066

Send a fax to 44 (0) 1865 314091

 Visit the Heinemann Bookshop at www.heinemann.co.uk/library to browse our catalogue and order online.

Produced by Roger Coote Publishing
Gissing's Farm, Fressingfield, Suffolk IP21 5SH, UK

First published in Great Britain by Heinemann Library, Halley Court, Jordan Hill, Oxford OX2 8EJ, part of Harcourt Education.
Heinemann is a registered trademark of Harcourt Education Ltd.

Editorial: Katie Orchard
Design: Jane Hawkins
Picture Research: Lynda Lines
Consultant: Dr Rachel Joce, Consultant in
  Communicable Disease Control
Production: Viv Hichens

Originated by Ambassador Litho Ltd
Printed and bound in China by South China
  Printing Company

ISBN 0 431 09818 2
07 06 05 04 03
10 9 8 7 6 5 4 3 2 1

British Library Cataloguing in Publication Data
Mason, Paul
  Body piercing and tattooing. - (Need to know)
  1.Body piercing - Juvenile literature 2.Tattooing -
  Juvenile literature
  I.Title
  391.6'5

Acknowledgements
The publishers would like to thank the following for permission to reproduce photographs:
AKG pp. 9, 36 (Norman Rockwell); Associated Press pp. 25 (Brian Bohannon), 29 (Tony Gutierrez), 37 (Douglas Pizac); Corbis pp. 5 (Tim Mosenfelder), 8 (Archivo Iconografico, S.A.), 13 (Horace Bristol), 14 (Bettman), 42 (Peter M. Fisher); C. M. Dixon p. 10; John Walmsley Photography p. 6; Medipics pp. 26–27 (Malcolm Earl), 34, 35; MPM Images *front cover (foreground)* (Daniel Rogers); Popperfoto pp. 12, 43 (Reinhard Kreuse/Reuters), 47 (John Reynolds); Rex Features pp. 4 (Suzanne Murphy), 7 (Richard Young), 17 (Richard Young), 19 (Tony Savino); 20 (Nils Jorgensen), 21 (Nils Jorgensen), 22–23 (Cesare Bonazza), 31 (Sipa), 33 (Eva Magazine), 38 (Tim Coleman), 41 (Chat Magazine), 44 (Mike Alsford), 45 (Nils Jorgensen), 50–51 (Tony Savino), *front cover (background)* (Tony Savino); Science Photo Library pp. 32 (Dr P. Marazzi), 48–49 (Hank Morgan); Topham Picturepoint p. 24.

Every effort has been made to contact copyright holders of any material reproduced in this book. Any omissions will be rectified in subsequent printings if notice is given to the publishers.

Any words appearing in the text in bold, **like this**, are explained in the Glossary.

Contents

Piercing and tattooing

Body piercing and tattooing have probably never been as popular as they are today. Tattoos especially seem to be everywhere – actresses from Roseanne Barr to Drew Barrymore, musicians such as Mary J. Blige and Eminem, and athletes such as Dennis Rodman, David Beckham and Mark Philippoussis, all have tattoos.

Piercings can be harder to spot – often they are hidden under clothes – but you only have to walk down a high street in London, New York or Sydney to see a variety of people with nose studs, navel rings, and pierced eyebrows and tongues.

Less than 50 years ago in the West, body piercing and tattooing were nowhere near as common. Teenagers in the 1950s and early 1960s, for example, would have found it much more difficult to get piercings and tattoos than they do today. For one thing, there were far fewer tattoo parlours and piercing studios. For another, people had a very different view of piercings and tattoos. One woman who was a teenager in the 1960s remembered: 'I desperately wanted to have my ears pierced. It seems nothing today, but at the time it was a very big deal. My mother told me – very clearly and many times – that having your ears pierced was "common" and "sluttish". She made it pretty clear that if I came home with pierced ears I might as well pack my bags and leave, as I'd have brought shame on the whole family.'

This woman wears a piercing in her nose as part of her costume.

Pierced noses, eyebrows, navels and other body parts were so unusual that most people would have been amazed to hear about them. Tattoos were more common than piercings after the Second World War, but were mainly associated with men serving in the Army or Navy.

In the recent past – even twenty years ago – piercings and tattoos were seen as a way of rebelling against polite society, so it is easy to think that they have always been like that. This is not the case: from **Polynesian** chiefs to the cream of Edwardian society, from the rain forests of South America to the household of Queen Victoria, body piercing and tattooing have a long and varied history.

"One must *be* a work of art, or *wear* a work of art."

(Oscar Wilde)

Soul diva Mary J. Blige is one of many musicians who sport tattoos.

What are piercing and tattooing?

Body piercing

Body piercing involves pushing a sharp object through a person's skin, so that it goes under the outer layer and comes back out through the skin in a different place. Various objects – today usually metal jewellery – can then be put into the hole to keep it open. After a while the flesh around the hole heals up naturally, and the jewellery can then be changed.

Soft flesh – an earlobe, for example – is most suitable for piercing, but almost any part of the body can be pierced. Noses, eyebrows, cheeks, nipples, navels, lips, tongues – all these and more are pierced by fans of body piercing. Why people choose to have their body pierced is much harder to explain than how it is done.

Many people have piercings done as a kind of body adornment or decoration – eyebrow rings among Western teenagers, for example, are purely decorative. In some cultures a piercing may have a special significance, such as showing that a boy has reached maturity and become a man.

Tattooing

Tattooing is the practice of making a visible design under someone's skin. Tattoos are made by putting ink through the outer layer of skin, into the layer beneath. This second layer, which is known as the **dermis**, moves very little during a person's lifetime and does not break down, so tattoos are **permanent**.

There are various ways of getting tattoo ink into the flesh, but all involve piercing or cutting the skin. Today this is usually done using an electric-powered device that pushes a needle up and down, piercing the skin on each downstroke and injecting a small amount of ink into the flesh.

Most people's tattoos have special significance to them, making each tattoo personal to the individual.

Other, less permanent, tattoo-like skin markings are also sometimes used. These include henna tattoos and transfers, which are applied to the skin and eventually rub off.

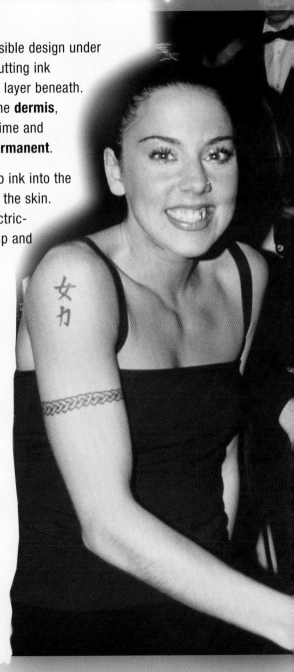

Mel C. from the Spice Girls has a tattoo in Chinese characters meaning 'girl power' or, literally, 'woman' and 'strength'. Her mother has the same tattoo.

History of body piercing

Piercing has been practised around the world for many centuries. Sometimes people in the past were pierced purely for personal reasons: Cleopatra, for example, is said to have had one of her nipples pierced because it was inverted. She did not like the way it looked, so had the nipple pierced and would put a tiny, smooth stone in the hole to make her nipple stick out.

Coming of age

Other piercings have been done as a way of marking a significant event in someone's life: the moment when a boy became a man, for example, or when a woman got married. In Central Africa, ancient tribal customs suggested that a woman would be more valuable as a wife if she had had a particular piercing. Girls who were about to become women attended a special ceremony at which the piercing was performed. The ceremony included a **symbolic** sacrifice of their girlhood, or virginity.

This Ancient Egyptian bust shows that people were wearing earrings at least 4000 years ago.

Portable currency

One type of piercing was done as a way of storing wealth. In the days of sailing ships sailors needed to store their money in a way that was both easily available and useable in any country at which their ship called. So they had their ears pierced, and into the piercing went a gold ring. Gold could then be shaved off or added to the ring as needed, and gold could buy goods in whichever port the ships docked.

A Roman gladiator. Some gladiators were known to have piercings.

Protective piercings

Gladiators in the Roman arenas are said to have had the ends of their penises pierced, for two reasons. First, to stop them having children with lower-class women (rich women are said to have sometimes paid to have the children of famous gladiators). Unless the penis ring was released it was impossible for the gladiators to have sex. Secondly, a gladiator who fought naked could strap his penis against his leg to keep it out of the way of swinging blades, spears and other weapons.

Fashion victims

In Britain many Victorian gentlemen felt that their trousers would hang better if everything could be kept smart below the waistline. Some apparently had their penises pierced with a ring so that they could be held in a position that wouldn't spoil the look of the latest fashionable trousers. Even Prince Albert, the husband of Queen Victoria, is alleged to have had his penis pierced.

History of tattoos

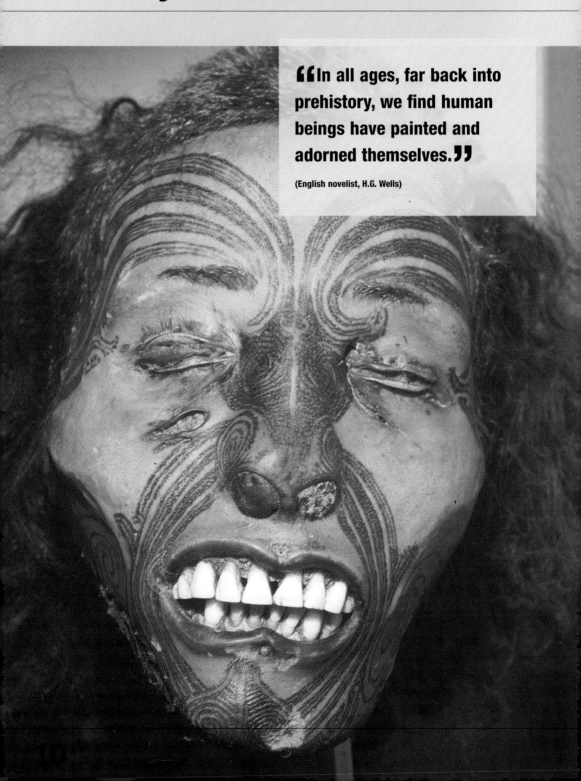

"In all ages, far back into prehistory, we find human beings have painted and adorned themselves."

(English novelist, H.G. Wells)

No one knows for certain when the first tattoo was done. Skin usually rots away after death, so it is very difficult to know when tattoos were first made. Evidence of ancient tattoos has come mainly from places where bodies have been **mummified**, preserving their skin and leaving behind the design that the mummified person wore in life.

Preserved skin

In 1993 an ancient mummified body was discovered in a high, windswept area of Siberia, in Russia, known as the Pastures of Heaven. The mummy was of a woman, who became known as the Ice Maiden. In life she had been a priestess. Probably because of this, her skin was covered in bright blue tattoos of animal figures, representing the creatures her people would have relied on for food. The Ice Maiden had been frozen in the Siberian ice for over 2400 years, making her one of the oldest known tattooed ladies. There is evidence that Ancient Egyptians had tattoos even earlier than the Ice Maiden, in about 2000 BCE.

Left: The mummified head of this Maori chief shows the face tattoos he wore in life.

And in 1992 a mummified, tattooed man's body was found in the European Alps, on the border between Italy and Austria. The Ice Man, as he became known, had been buried in a **glacier** for roughly 4000 years, making his tattoos as old as the Ancient Egyptian ones.

Tattooed warriors

About 2000 years after the Ice Man was first buried in his glacier, invading Roman armies reached northern Britain. There they encountered Pict warriors, who lived in the area that is now Scotland. The Pict fighters were covered in blue tattoos, and were so fierce that the **Roman legions** could not subdue them. Instead the Romans were forced to build Hadrian's Wall along the northern border of England, to keep out their tattooed enemies.

The purposes of these ancient tattoos are not certain. They may have been purely for decoration, but are more likely to have been a sign of a person's rank, or position. Having a tattoo today can be painful; it may have been more so then, and tattooing would have been a dangerous process because of the risk of a cut becoming infected.

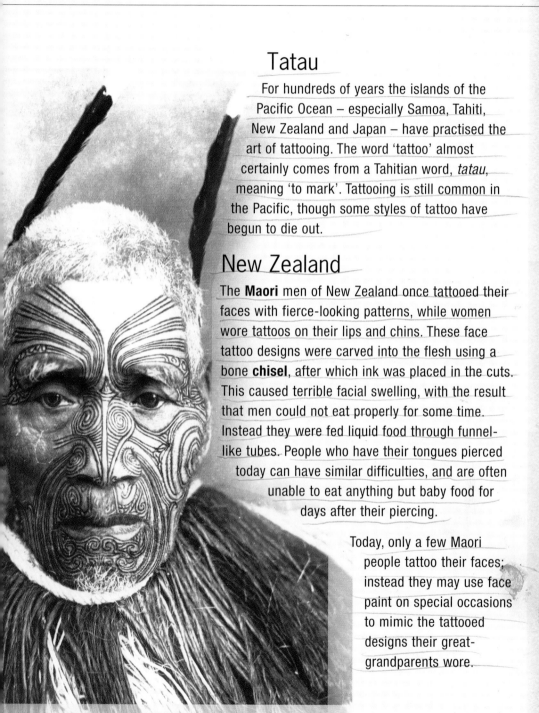

Tatau

For hundreds of years the islands of the Pacific Ocean – especially Samoa, Tahiti, New Zealand and Japan – have practised the art of tattooing. The word 'tattoo' almost certainly comes from a Tahitian word, *tatau*, meaning 'to mark'. Tattooing is still common in the Pacific, though some styles of tattoo have begun to die out.

New Zealand

The **Maori** men of New Zealand once tattooed their faces with fierce-looking patterns, while women wore tattoos on their lips and chins. These face tattoo designs were carved into the flesh using a bone **chisel**, after which ink was placed in the cuts. This caused terrible facial swelling, with the result that men could not eat properly for some time. Instead they were fed liquid food through funnel-like tubes. People who have their tongues pierced today can have similar difficulties, and are often unable to eat anything but baby food for days after their piercing.

Today, only a few Maori people tattoo their faces; instead they may use face paint on special occasions to mimic the tattooed designs their great-grandparents wore.

Samoa

On the Samoan islands, tattooing was a mark of a man's ability to bear pain. This is still true today, and not just for Samoan men! In Samoan society a man without tattoos would have been thought a complete weakling.

Samoan tattoos were applied using a special comb. The teeth of the comb were dipped in ink then tapped into the skin, puncturing it and leaving the ink in the flesh beneath. A complicated design could take as long as six months to finish, and was applied in a specially built tattooing hut. Once the tattoo was finished, the hut would be burnt.

Japan

Japanese tattoos are famous, incorporating many different colours to create some of the most intricate designs in the world. Traditionally, people who had full-body tattoos in Japan belonged almost entirely to an organized group of criminals called *yakuza*. Even a simple Japanese carp tattoo on a person's shoulder can take months to finish, and full-body tattoos have always taken years to complete.

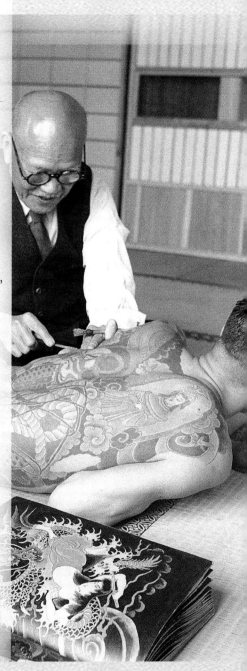

Many *yakuza* had tattoos that covered their entire bodies, ending only at the neck, wrists and ankles.

Into the West

Although people in ancient Europe had once tattooed themselves, the practice had largely died out by the 17th century. Then, in 1769, Captain Cook's voyage through the Pacific brought his sailors into contact with tattooing. Some of Cook's men brought home a **permanent** souvenir of their visit to the South Seas in the form of a tattoo.

"A sailor without a tattoo is like a ship without grog [alcohol]: not seaworthy."

(Samuel O'Reilly, a famous New York City tattoo artist)

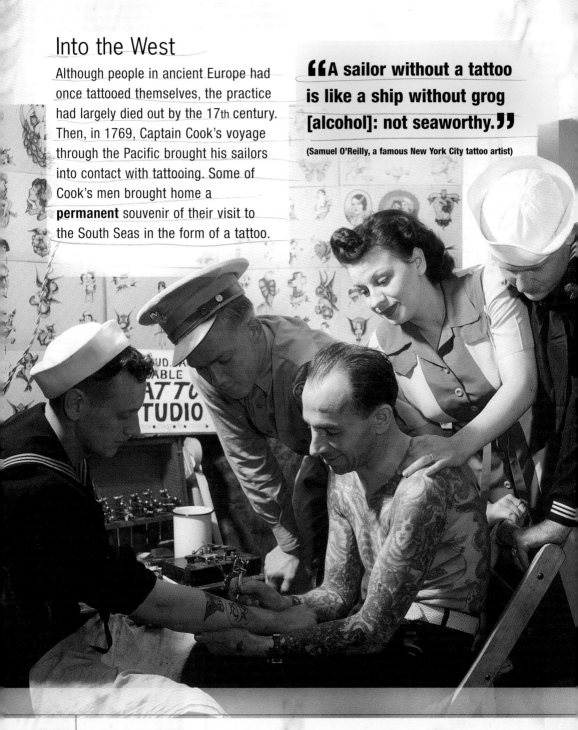

At the time, sailors were just about the toughest, most unruly and uncontrollable people around. Ever since Cook's explorations, tattoos have been associated with sailors. This is perhaps the reason tattoos gained a disreputable image.

People in Europe and North America became fascinated by tattoos. During the eighteenth and nineteenth centuries, tattooed Indians or Pacific Islanders drew great crowds of people who were willing to pay to see their unusual skin markings. It was not long before an increasing number of tattooists began to set up shop, offering to give people tattoos. Their best customers were sailors and soldiers – far fewer people from outside the armed forces wanted to have tattoos.

During the nineteenth and twentieth centuries many people looked down on tattoos, thinking them a sign that someone was badly behaved and **anti-social**.

Left: Yet another tattoo is added to a sailor's already colourful skin in a New York tattoo studio.

The US government even tried to limit tattoos among the armed forces – 1909 recruitment regulations stated: 'indecent or obscene tattooing is cause for rejection.' This regulation caused a mini-boom in the tattooing industry in the 1940s, as young men flocked to have clothes put on their rude tattoos so that they could join up to fight in the Second World War.

The Great Omi

Perhaps the strangest tattooed person ever was a fairground star called 'The Great Omi'. Omi – whose real name, Horace Ridler, was known only to a tiny number of people during his lifetime – had been an officer in the British Army, and came from a respectable, middle-class background. A series of financial disasters left him almost penniless, and he decided to turn himself into a **freak-show** star. Starting in 1927, the Great Omi was tattooed all over to look like a zebra. The tattoos on Omi's face and head alone required 15,000,000 needle pricks, and the entire process took over a year. His tattooist noted dryly, and with massive understatement, that the tattooing 'must have caused some pain and distress'.

Motivations

Today there is usually more than one reason behind a person's decision to have a tattoo or piercing. People give many different reasons for deciding to modify or decorate their body in some way.

Rebellion

Years ago almost the only people who had tattoos were the tough and uncontrollable: sailors, soldiers, **Hell's Angels** and criminals. Having a tattoo marked a person as an outsider, someone who did not play by the rules. Tattoos and piercings are still unusual enough for people who have them to be seen as rebels. People who are especially heavily tattooed or pierced look different: they have rebelled against the usual rules about how a person should look.

Rites of passage

A rite of passage is a ceremony or event that marks a change or turning point in someone's life: becoming an adult or getting married, for example. The actress Pamela Anderson once said that 'tattoos are **symbolic** of the most important moments of your life'.

Of course, as time goes by, tattoos and piercings can take on a different meaning. Pamela realized this herself, when she imagined the day when: 'my sons' first girlfriends come over and I'm all wrinkled up in a chair with tattoos all sagging down to my ankles.'

Aspirations

Some people use tattoos as a way of showing what they are aiming for. Several sportsmen and women, for example, have had **Olympic rings** tattooed on their bodies to show how much they want to compete in the Olympic Games.

Love

Some people have the names of their loved ones tattooed on their skin. This is not without risk: 'Mum' and 'Dad' are pretty safe, but other loved ones can change. Almost all professional

> **❝I go all the time now – once every four months. It's very addictive.❞**
>
> **(US comedienne, Roseanne Barr)**

tattooists can tell stories about people asking to have the name of a former boyfriend or girlfriend covered up with a new design.

Sadness

Sometimes a tattoo or piercing is done to remember a sad event: the death of a friend, for example. The actress Alyssa Milano once said 'I've always gotten them [tattoos] at times when I was sad about something [...] relationship problems or the fact that it had rained every day for a month.'

No significance!

People don't always have a reason for getting a tattoo or piercing done other than that it looked good or felt right. Lots of people say that once they had one, they couldn't help going back for more.

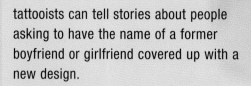

Tomb Raider actress Angelina Jolie had Billy Bob Thornton's name tattooed on her arm soon after she married him. But by the summer of 2002 the two were reported to have split up. This made Angelina's tattoo a match for Billy Bob's own tattoo of an earlier wife's name.

How tattooing works

Tattooing involves placing ink under the outer layer of skin, into the **dermis**. The cells of the dermis are very stable, so ink that is added to them stays almost exactly where it is for as long as the skin is alive.

Around the world, various methods have been used for tattooing, including needles, knives, **chisels**, and a needle and thread. But in 1891 Samuel O'Reilly transformed the art of tattooing with his new, electric-powered invention – the first automatic tattoo machine. Based on Thomas Edison's Electric Pen, O'Reilly's device had a needle that moved up and down like a mini-jackhammer, carrying ink into the skin with each downward stroke. Modern tattoo machines work in a similar way.

High-speed tattoos

Today's electric tattoo machines puncture the skin between 50 and 3000 times a minute. They use a **sterilized** needle, which drives tiny particles of ink about 3 mm deep into the dermis, before withdrawing to collect more ink. The ink travels to the needle through tubes. The machine is controlled using a foot pedal like the one on an ordinary sewing machine.

Almost all tattoos are done following a **stencil** or outline of the design. This is stuck to the skin, and allows the customer to say whether they want it bigger, smaller or in a different place. Some customers decide at this point that they do not want the tattoo done at all. One problem with home-made tattoos is that they are often done without a stencil, so the tattoo ends up looking badly drawn or in the wrong position.

Once the customer is happy with the size and position of the stencil, the actual tattoo is begun. First the skin is cleaned and prepared with antiseptic soap and water. Then the tattooist makes an outline of the design using a single needle, usually with black ink. Next the outline is thickened and the shading is added, still usually in black ink. The area is cleaned again, and then colour can be added. After being wiped clean a final time, the tattoo is complete.

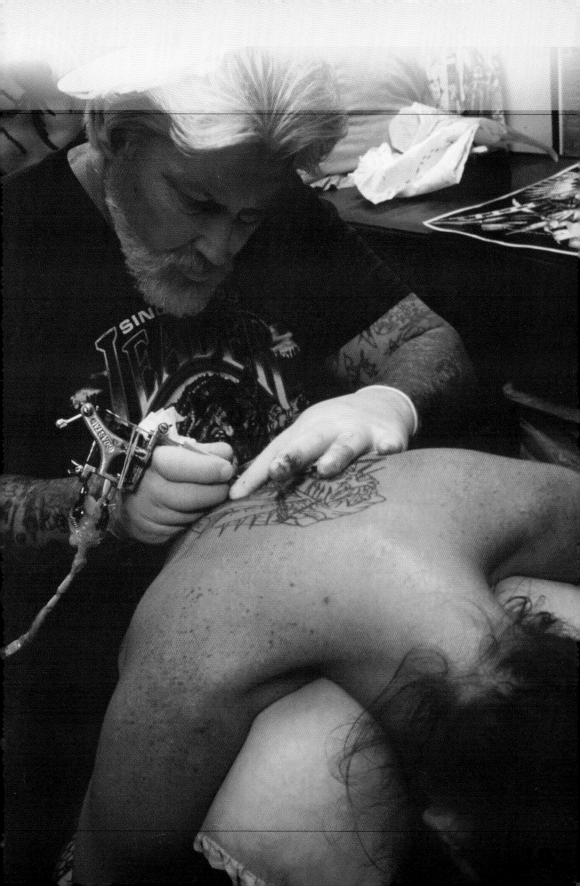

How piercing is done

Clamps are used to hold the skin in the correct position for piercing.

Piercing punctures the skin more deeply than tattooing, and is potentially more painful, although piercing is a far quicker process. Some piercings are like minor **surgery**, and occasionally an ethyl chloride spray is used to freeze the area before the piercing is made. Most piercings are performed without the use of any kind of painkiller.

The area to be pierced is pinched together, using clamps. Then a hollow needle in a plastic tube coated in **lubricant** is pushed through the skin and flesh by the piercer, hollowing out a passage. The needle is pulled out, leaving the plastic tube in the passage. Jewellery is then pushed into the tube. The tube is eased out of the **wound**, leaving only the jewellery behind.

In some places, such as hairdressing salons or beauticians' studios, piercings are done using an instrument called a **piercing gun**. This is a mechanical device loaded with a stud, which is used both to make the piercing and as the jewellery that keeps it open. The flesh to be pierced is placed inside the top of the gun, then the stud is lined up with the desired spot. The handle is pulled to release the stud and force it through the skin. A fastener is added to the stud on the exit side of the wound, to keep it in place. Professional piercers usually refuse to use piercing guns, which are potentially less **hygienic** than single-use hollow needles and can squash the area around the piercing site.

Piercing jewellery is usually made of highly polished surgical steel, which contains nickel. If the person being pierced has an **allergy** to nickel, jewellery made of titanium or 18-carat gold is used instead. Each of these

helps prevent the wound from becoming infected.

After the piercing is finished the wound is cleaned, and bandaged if necessary. Bandaging is normally used on a piercing where the surrounding flesh may move around a lot and cause further bleeding, for example a navel piercing. Many piercing studios will also give their customers written advice on how to care for their piercing.

A customer is shown her new piercing in a mirror.

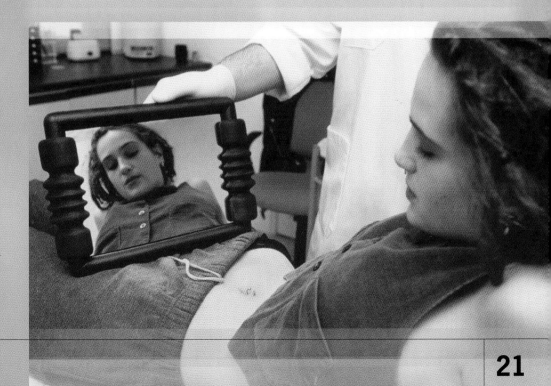

Cosmetic tattooing

A cosmetic tattoo is one that is done for reasons of personal appearance, almost like wearing make-up or having a haircut. The reasons for having cosmetic tattoos can be to have **permanent** make-up, or to hide a disfigurement or defect of some sort.

The earliest modern cosmetic tattooing was done in Britain, about 100 years ago. In the early 1900s it became fashionable for ladies of London Society to have healthy-looking flushed cheeks. One way for them to achieve this look was to wear make-up, but at the time this was thought of as unsuitable for smart ladies. Instead, some of the smartest and richest ladies in the country came to beauty salons to have colour tattooed on their cheeks. As one tattooist remembered in his memoirs: 'the word "tattooing" was never mentioned'. Instead, smart ladies came to the beauty salon where he worked to have a 'permanent beauty treatment'.

War veterans

After the First and Second World Wars, skilled tattooists worked alongside doctors, helping men who had suffered injuries during the fighting. Often the men's faces had been affected by heat or **shrapnel**, or discoloured by gunpowder blasts. Tattooing ink was used to bring the colour of their skin back to normal and make their injuries less noticeable.

A cosmetic tattooist carefully applies colour to a woman's lips.

Cosmetic tattooing today

For a time, cosmetic tattooing went out of fashion, as people became scared by the idea of **facial tattooing** in particular. After the First World War, the cosmetics industry began to persuade women that it was acceptable for them to wear make-up rather than having a 'permanent beauty treatment'. Today, however, cosmetic tattooing is making a comeback. It is used to outline eyebrows, or even replace them entirely if they have fallen out for some reason. Tattooing can even be used to make eyelashes look bigger and thicker, but the slightest mistake by the tattooist is disastrous. The tattooing is so close to the eye that it could easily be damaged, and the lid contains fine blood vessels, which the tattooist has to be careful to avoid.

Cosmetic tattooing can also be used to reduce **smallpox**- or **acne-pitting** of the skin, make thin hair look thicker, or even apply a permanent 'lipstick' to a woman's lips. Facial tattooing is illegal in many countries, and usually only a licensed medical practitioner can apply cosmetic tattoos.

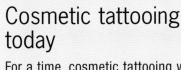

23

Does it hurt?

Tattoos and pain

Having a tattoo done will almost certainly hurt to some extent. People have claimed otherwise: 'Professor' George Burchett was one of the most famous tattooists, and tattooed Edwardian ladies, fairground performers and even King Frederik of Denmark. Burchett claimed that 'the normal tattooing operation is not painful – indeed, many of my clients have assured me that the "prickle" is pleasant'. Most people who have tattoos done admit it is, at best, uncomfortable, and can be extremely painful. Some people say that having a tattoo is like being snapped with a rubber band over and over again; others compare it to having pins and needles.

George Burchett (left) shows a client a tattoo that he designed for King Frederik of Denmark.

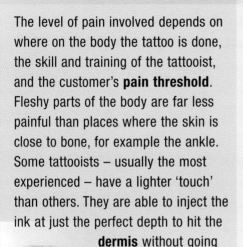

The level of pain involved depends on where on the body the tattoo is done, the skill and training of the tattooist, and the customer's **pain threshold**. Fleshy parts of the body are far less painful than places where the skin is close to bone, for example the ankle. Some tattooists – usually the most experienced – have a lighter 'touch' than others. They are able to inject the ink at just the perfect depth to hit the **dermis** without going too deep and causing pain.

Piercing and pain

The amount of pain involved in being pierced is hard to gauge because it depends on where the piercing is being done. Many people find that ear piercing is relatively painless, though afterwards the ears can throb for a while. Other piercings can be uncomfortable or even downright painful. Navel piercing, for example, goes through sensitive flesh and affects an area of the body that moves around a lot. The act of piercing the navel can be more painful than some other places, and the **wound** can be uncomfortable for a long time afterwards – it can take longer than a year for it to heal fully. The amount of pain also varies according to the skill of the piercer and how much pain the customer can withstand.

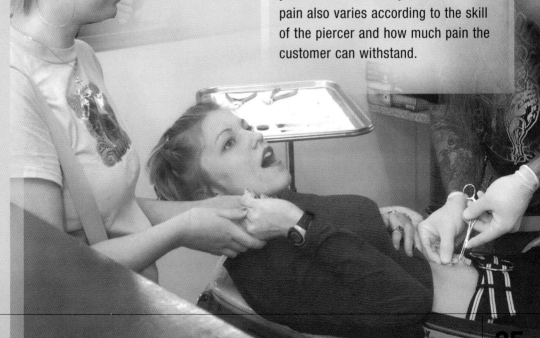

Safe tattoos and piercings

There are health risks involved in having a tattoo done or being pierced. Tattoo and piercing studios have to be very careful not to cause their customers harm. Reputable studios – the ones that have a proper store front and professional equipment – usually stick to the safety rules. They also ask their customers health-related questions before starting work. **Back-street** and mobile tattooists and body piercers may not be so careful. This means there is a greater risk of something going wrong. There are various signs that a tattoo or piercing studio uses proper safety procedures.

Disposables

Most pieces of equipment are used only once and then thrown away, to avoid the possibility of disease spreading from one person to the next. Disposable tattoo equipment includes ink, ink cups, gloves and tattoo needles. A good tattooist will show customers the new, unopened packages containing each of these before opening the seals on them in the customer's presence. The same is true of a professional piercer, who will break the seals on the needles in front of the customer. Piercing needles and the plastic tubes that surround them (which come in the same package) should be used only once, as should all antiseptic wipes and cloths.

Autoclaves such as this one are essential for keeping piercing and tattooing equipment as clean as possible.

Autoclaves

Items that are reused in the tattooing or piercing processes need to be cleaned then **sterilized** in an **autoclave** before they are used again. For tattooing these include the needle bar and the tube; for piercing the only reusables are the clamps used to hold the flesh in position. Using an autoclave is the only way of killing micro-organisms such as viruses or bacteria. Autoclaves work by heating the instruments to a very high temperature – sometimes as high as 132 °C. Some items go through the autoclave in a special pouch, and once they have reached the correct temperature an indicator strip on the pouch changes colour.

Safe tattoos and piercings

Pre-tattoo procedure

A good tattooist follows a careful procedure before starting a tattoo. He or she washes their hands, disinfects the work area and puts on a fresh pair of gloves. The spray bottles, which hold the ink, are then covered with plastic bags, and the tattooist should then explain the **sterilization** procedure. After this, he or she will break the seals on the sterilized **autoclave** equipment and the single-use items such as needles, in front of the customer. This ensures that everyone knows the correct equipment is being used. Once the skin has been washed and shaved to stop the needles getting clogged with hair, and the transfer of the design has been applied, the tattooing can begin. (See pages 18–19 for a description of the tattooing procedure.)

Pre-piercing procedure

Piercing involves fewer items of equipment than tattooing, so the pre-piercing procedure is less complicated. If the area being pierced is hairy, the hair is shaved off. Then the clamps are taken out of the autoclave, and the work area is wiped clean with antiseptic, antibacterial wipes. Two dots are drawn on the skin to show where the piercing will enter and come out of the flesh. Once the customer is happy, the seal can be broken on the needle, and the piercing can begin.

A piercer wearing sterile gloves collects equipment together on a tray, before beginning the piercing procedure.

Possible problems

Home-made tattoos

A study by the Children's Medical Center at the University of Massachusetts, USA, suggests that most teenagers get tattoos done by their friends, using pens, paper clips and other unsuitable items. The risks involved in having this type of tattoo are relatively high. A tattoo done by a friend with little or no experience is unlikely to turn out as planned, which can lead to the loss of a friendship as well as an unwanted tattoo.

Home-made tattoos are also likely to be painful, because the tattooist will not know how far under the skin the ink has to be placed and may go too deep. There is a good chance that a home-made tattoo will become infected because the equipment used has not been **sterilized**.

❝Soup for three weeks – it was all I could eat, my tongue was so swollen.❞

(Alex Johnson, 19, speaking about the effects of having a pierced tongue)

Passing on blood-borne viruses

There are risks of passing on blood-borne viruses, both in tattooing and body piercing. The American Academy of Dermatology has recorded cases of blood-borne viruses, such as **hepatitis B**, being passed from one person to the next when equipment is not sterilized before being used. People carrying these viruses in their blood do not necessarily look ill, and may not even be aware of the fact that they have a virus. Even if someone looks healthy they may not be, so using clean and safe equipment is always crucial.

HIV and hepatitis C

There are no definite cases of **HIV** or **hepatitis C** being passed on through tattooing, although the risk does exist. Because the needles used are solid, not hollow like a syringe, passing on HIV or hepatitis C through tattooing is unlikely. By 2000, the Center for Disease Control and Prevention in the USA had not recorded any confirmed cases.

The possibility of HIV or hepatitis C being passed on through piercing is theoretically far higher, since the needles used are hollow and offer a hiding place for the virus to survive. In a professional studio, only disposable needles should be used. **Back-street** and mobile piercing studios are unlikely to have the same standards of **hygiene**.

Tahitian turtles

Even today, not all tattoos are done using modern equipment. The actress Gillian Anderson, who stars in *The X-Files*, has a small tattoo of a pair of turtles on her ankle. It was done in Tahiti, and Anderson recalls: '[The tattooist's] equipment was a sewing needle attached to an old electric razor, with a ballpoint pen casing with a shish-kebab stick through it… It was painful. It felt like I was at the dentist and they were drilling into my bone.' Makeshift equipment like this is not only painful; it carries the risk of serious infection, because it is far less likely to be kept clean than proper modern tattooing machines.

Possible problems

Post-procedure infections

In both tattooing and body piercing there is a risk of infection setting in after the tattoo or piercing is finished. This is why it is important to make sure everything is clean and **hygienic**. This is especially true in piercing. A navel piercing, for example, can take up to a year to heal fully. Unless a piercing is kept properly clean, the **wound** is likely to become infected. The surrounding flesh may swell up and the wound may start to weep fluid. If left unchecked, the flesh will start to grow against the jewellery, sealing it into the skin. At this point, the only way to remove the jewellery is to cut it out through minor **surgery**. Ear piercings can lead to an infection of the ear's cartilage, causing scarring.

Allergic reactions

It is possible to have an **allergic reaction** to the ink that is used in tattooing. None of the 50 or so colours used in tattooing are **regulated** by the US Food and Drug Administration, for example, so there are few guarantees that they have been fully tested as safe. The inks that were traditionally used in tattooing contained resins, acrylic, glycerol or all three, but tattooists are now increasingly using **organic** pigments as colours, in an attempt to avoid allergic reactions.

Piercing problems

Special problems can be caused if someone whose body is still growing has a piercing. The flesh surrounding a fourteen-year-old's navel, for example, is likely to change its shape over the next few years. If it is pierced, the hole made by the piercing is likely to change shape, too, possibly becoming uncomfortable and making it difficult to put jewellery inside.

Inexperienced piercers may pierce either too deep into the flesh or not deep enough. Eyebrow piercing, for example, is done at a depth of 12 mm. The healing process contracts the piercing slightly, bringing the depth to about 10 mm. A piercing made at a lesser depth will contract to such a shallow depth that the surrounding skin will start to reject it and the piercing will grow out. Piercings that have been made too deeply carry different problems: they 'bunch' around the hole, making an ugly lump, and are uncomfortable and slow-healing as a result.

Other problems can also occur. The jewellery from tongue piercings can damage tooth enamel, painfully and sometimes **permanently**. Navel piercings can cause difficulties for women during pregnancy, as the skin around their stomach swells and the piercing becomes stretched out of shape.

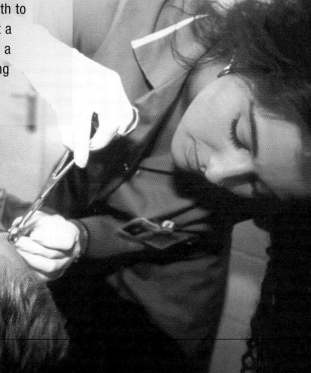

Caring for tattoos and piercings

Once a tattoo has been finished, it needs to be looked after carefully: there can be health problems if it has not healed properly, and the design can blur. All tattoos bleed slightly just after they are finished. This bleeding normally stops within a few minutes, but if the person being tattooed has been drinking alcohol or taking certain drugs, or has been tattooed over a scar, bleeding can continue.

A healing tattoo

A new tattoo is bandaged in the tattoo studio. The bandage needs to be removed about two hours later. The tattoo is then washed gently in mild antibacterial soap and patted dry. Rubbing dry a new tattoo can cause the colours and shape to blur. Then a very thin coat of ointment is gently worked into the skin: too much of this could pull the colour out of the skin, and most tattooists warn that if it is possible to see the ointment on the skin, too much is being used.

While a tattoo is healing, which usually takes between one and three weeks, it needs to be kept dry as much as possible. Letting the shower

New tattoos are often sore and inflamed just after being finished.

pound down on it, soaking in a hot bath, and swimming in the sea or pools can all cause problems. Sometimes a scab forms on a tattoo, which falls off on its own when the tattoo has healed. Any sign of infection must be treated by a doctor.

Caring for a piercing

Caring for a new piercing mainly involves keeping it clean, especially until it has fully healed. The piercing has to be washed in the morning and evening with antibacterial soap. As soon as it is bearable, the jewellery keeping the **wound** open should be turned to prevent it from being sealed against the flesh. This routine needs to be followed until the piercing is completely healed, when all swelling and tenderness have disappeared. Once the wound has healed completely, it should still be cleaned regularly, using soap and possibly cotton buds if the hole is large enough.

A new navel piercing is cleaned with a cotton bud and antibacterial liquid.

Permanence

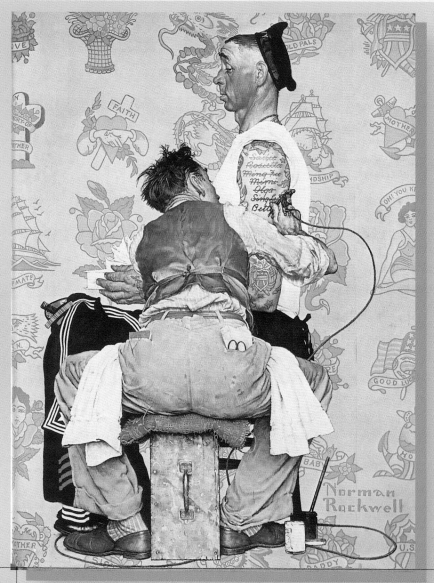

Tattoos are **permanent**. They are made by placing ink in a stable layer of skin, which does not break down. Unless the ink is removed in some way, the tattoo stays where it is for ever. Until the late 1980s the only way to remove a tattoo was to cut away the skin in which it was embedded. This was a painful procedure that left bad scarring.

The American Academy of Dermatology estimates that between 1979 and 1999 the number of registered tattoo studios in the USA grew from 300 to over 4000. This growth has been matched in many other Western countries. As the number of people getting tattoos has grown, so has the number of people wanting to have their tattoos removed. A whole new technique has been developed, using lasers to remove unwanted tattoos.

Laser removal

Lasers remove tattoos by **vaporizing** (heating to a temperature where they disappear) the colours in the tattooing ink, using a high-intensity beam of light. One big problem with the laser removal of tattoos is the expense. A medium-sized tattoo costing about £50 to have made costs between £800 and £1200 to remove. (For more information about laser removal, see pages 48–49.)

Permanent holes

Most piercings are also permanent. Once a piercing has healed it will rarely fully close up. However, a piercing without jewellery in it is not as noticeable as a tattoo, and can be more easily forgotten about.

Left: In this painting by the American artist Norman Rockwell, a sailor has the name of yet another girlfriend crossed out when a new one is added!

Right: Holes left by piercings are usually inconspicuous unless they contain jewellery, but some holes can be enlarged to become very noticeable.

Impermanent tattoos

These feet have been patterned with henna, which wears off in about a week.

For anyone not 100 per cent sure that they want a tattoo that will be with them for the rest of their life, there are less-than-**permanent** options. These include **temporary** tattoos that are stuck to the skin, henna tattoos that stain the outer layer of skin, and tattoos using ink that breaks down and disappears over a period of time.

Temporary tattoos

Temporary tattoos are transfers that are added to the skin using water. The transfer is placed flat against the skin, then soaked in water. As the backing paper moistens it can be peeled away, leaving just the tattoo design on the skin. Temporary tattoos last up to seven days.

One of the advantages of temporary tattoos is that as well as buying pre-designed transfers it is possible to make up personal designs, using kits available in some shops and over the Internet. People who are thinking about having a permanent tattoo can make up the design they want as a temporary tattoo and wear it for up to seven days as a way of getting used to it. If the temporary tattoo no longer looks good to them after a week, they can decide not to have it done.

Henna tattoos

Henna tattoos use a plant extract to stain the surface of the skin, usually a dark brown colour. These tattoos are temporary, and wear away as the surface of the skin is worn away and replaced with new skin. Henna designs are an ancient tradition, especially among people from the Indian subcontinent and the Middle East. Women wear complicated designs on their hands and feet, often to mark special occasions. A woman who is about to get married may have very elaborate designs that take many hours to apply.

Disappearing tattoos

Tattoos that last only a certain period of time before fading away and disappearing are now available. They are made in the same way as a permanent tattoo, by injecting ink or pigment into a lower layer of the skin, but the ink used breaks up and fades away in a period of three to five years.

Making decisions

Given the **permanence** of piercings and tattoos, anyone considering either should think very hard about what they're about to do. A tattoo of a cartoon character or the name of a rock band might be fashionable now, but at the age of 50 will it just be an embarrassment? Anyone who does go ahead with a tattoo needs to be very sure that it is what they want, and that the significance of the tattoo will stay with them for the rest of their life.

Piercing is in some ways less of a long-term issue than tattooing, because if the jewellery is taken out it is less obvious. However, the social reactions to a visible piercing in an unusual place can be similar to tattoos, and some people want little or nothing to do with those who have obvious piercings. They may find piercings ugly, or not wish to be associated with someone who has marked themselves out as different from most others. The scars are also visible for a long time, and a lot of facial piercing can affect a person's appearance dramatically.

Experts suggest that people follow certain guidelines to avoid being stuck with a tattoo or piercing they do not like or which causes problems later:

- People should never get tattooed or pierced while drunk or after taking drugs. Not only will they be unable to make clear decisions, there are increased physical risks from prolonged bleeding.

- If possible they should try out the tattoo or piercing before getting it done permanently. This is easier for a tattoo, as there are kits available that let people make a **temporary** version of the design they want. For piercing people should spend some time imagining what effect the piercing will have: would an eyebrow piercing catch on glasses, or a nose piercing create difficulties during a cold, for example?

- People should consider the possible effect of having a tattoo or piercing on career prospects. Will it make a person less successful as a lawyer later on if they have the name of a band tattooed on their neck?

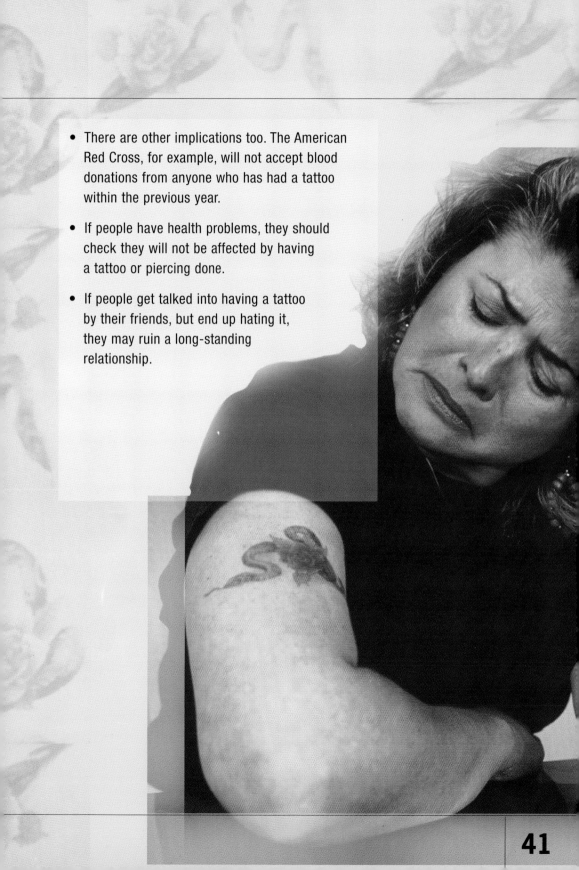

- There are other implications too. The American Red Cross, for example, will not accept blood donations from anyone who has had a tattoo within the previous year.

- If people have health problems, they should check they will not be affected by having a tattoo or piercing done.

- If people get talked into having a tattoo by their friends, but end up hating it, they may ruin a long-standing relationship.

Positive reactions

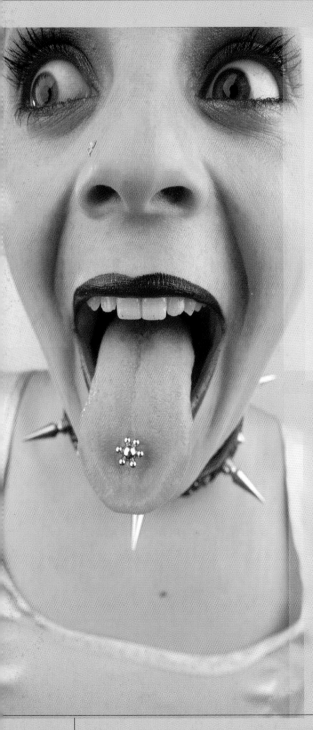

For many people, having a tattoo or a piercing is an uplifting experience. Usually they have thought long and hard about why they want it done, and have a special reason behind their decision. Once the tattoo or piercing is finished it becomes part of them, something that has an important place in their life.

Of course, some things that seem important now will not seem as important in ten years' time. The trick is telling one from the other. People who get this decision wrong often come to regret it later.

Memorial tattoos

On 13 February 1997 a professional surfer called Todd Chesser was killed in a big-wave surfing accident. Chesser was surfing with friends off the North Shore of the Hawaiian island, Oahu. The waves were enormous: Chesser drowned when he was held underwater for too long after falling from his surfboard. Chesser was one of the most popular surfers in Hawaii. His closest friends decided they would have tattoos done to remember him. Several of the world's best surfers now have tattoos with the words, 'In Loving Memory of Todd Chesser'.

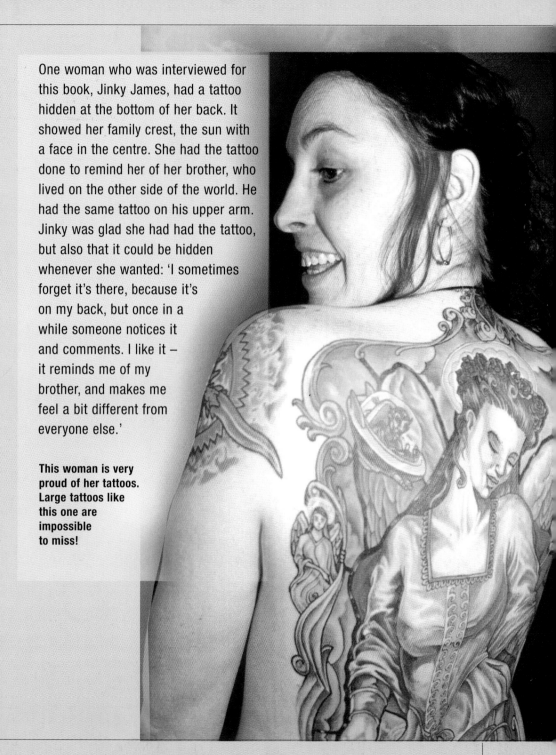

One woman who was interviewed for this book, Jinky James, had a tattoo hidden at the bottom of her back. It showed her family crest, the sun with a face in the centre. She had the tattoo done to remind her of her brother, who lived on the other side of the world. He had the same tattoo on his upper arm. Jinky was glad she had had the tattoo, but also that it could be hidden whenever she wanted: 'I sometimes forget it's there, because it's on my back, but once in a while someone notices it and comments. I like it – it reminds me of my brother, and makes me feel a bit different from everyone else.'

This woman is very proud of her tattoos. Large tattoos like this one are impossible to miss!

Negative reactions

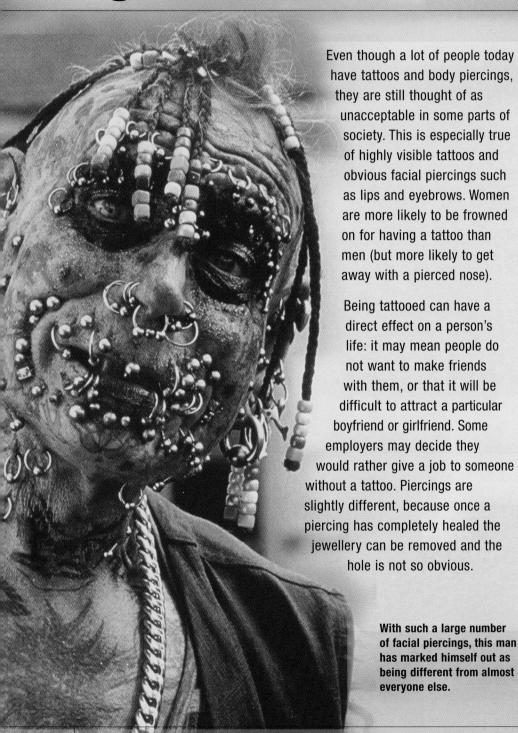

Even though a lot of people today have tattoos and body piercings, they are still thought of as unacceptable in some parts of society. This is especially true of highly visible tattoos and obvious facial piercings such as lips and eyebrows. Women are more likely to be frowned on for having a tattoo than men (but more likely to get away with a pierced nose).

Being tattooed can have a direct effect on a person's life: it may mean people do not want to make friends with them, or that it will be difficult to attract a particular boyfriend or girlfriend. Some employers may decide they would rather give a job to someone without a tattoo. Piercings are slightly different, because once a piercing has completely healed the jewellery can be removed and the hole is not so obvious.

With such a large number of facial piercings, this man has marked himself out as being different from almost everyone else.

Tattoo position

The position of a tattoo can be important. For example, a small design at the base of a person's spine is easily hidden: they can wear practically any clothes they like and the tattoo will remain tucked away unless it is deliberately revealed. A large tattoo on someone's chest, arms or legs (like the ones on the right) is harder to hide, especially in summer. If the tattoo needs to be hidden, all kinds of clothes suddenly become off-limits.

Regrets

Some people who have had tattoos done may regret it later. There is a whole industry based around tattoo removal, and many tattooists are asked to adapt old tattoos to say or show something different. Most of the people who later regret their tattoos had them done when they were young, on impulse, while they were drunk or by a friend.

Dexter Smith

Dexter Smith is a TV producer. He had a tattoo when he was 16 and at the time he was delighted with it. The tattoo is on his left shoulder and shows a small cartoon character. 'It now looks rubbish', says Dexter, 'the colours have all run together because I was still growing when I had it done and they've stretched, and it looks like a blob. I wish I'd had it done later, I wish it was of something – anything! – other than what it's of, and most of all I wish I hadn't had it done at all.'

Getting help

Tattoos and piercings can go wrong. They may become infected later, or a person might decide that they no longer want a tattoo or piercing, and need advice about how to get rid of it.

Immediate problems

When a tattoo or piercing becomes infected it will develop some or all of the following signs:
• redness and soreness
• swelling
• high temperature
• discharge of blood or pus oozing from the tattooed or pierced area
• in the case of a piercing, the jewellery may become 'stuck' and sealed into place.
If an infection develops, the only person who can provide proper help is a qualified medical professional.

Later problems

If any problems set in later – if a person becomes worried that they may have contracted a disease such as **HIV**, **hepatitis B** or **hepatitis C** through **unhygienic** conditions, for example – it is important to see a doctor as soon as possible.
A person who has developed a disease as a result of getting a tattoo or piercing done will need further medical treatment. Their doctor will be able to send them to the appropriate **specialist** or **counsellor** for further help. Customers are highly unlikely to catch a disease in a tattooing or piercing studio that follows health procedures, according to the Center for Disease Control and Prevention in the USA. **Back-street** and mobile studios, and tattoos and piercings that have been done by friends without the proper health procedures, offer a far higher possibility of infection, as such people may not have the same standards of **hygiene** and equipment as professional tattooists and piercers.

People who have decided that they no longer want their tattoo can go to discuss this with their doctor, who will be able to talk to them about the options. Usually the most realistic choice is simply to live with the tattoo, as the cost of having it removed is extremely high (see page 37). However, people who have **facial tattooing** may be able to get help, either through counselling or removal.

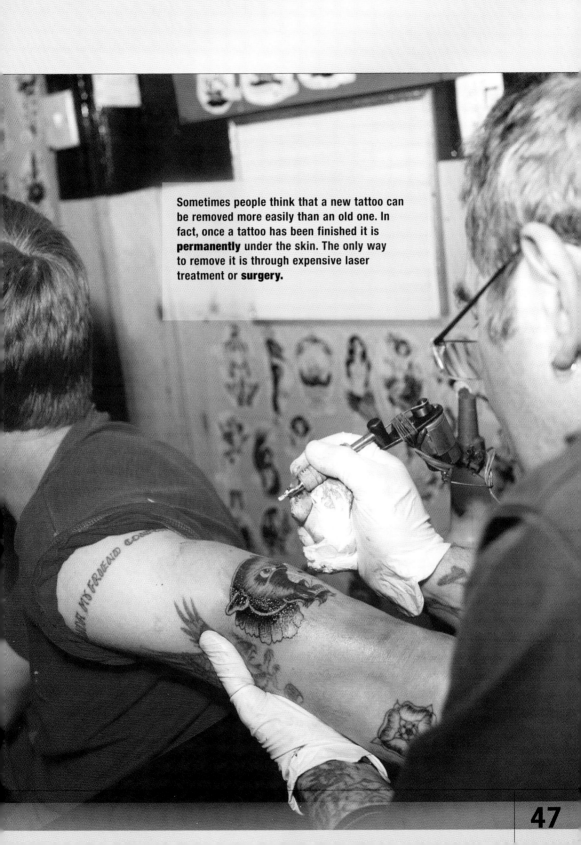

Sometimes people think that a new tattoo can be removed more easily than an old one. In fact, once a tattoo has been finished it is **permanently** under the skin. The only way to remove it is through expensive laser treatment or **surgery.**

Treatment and removal

Someone with a piercing they no longer want can deal with it relatively easily. If they take out the jewellery inside the piercing, usually all that is visible will be a small hole at the entrance and exit of the piercing. This hole is likely to be **permanent**, and cannot be filled in except by tissue regrowing naturally in the hole. But in most cases the holes left by a piercing are usually hard to see, and easy to ignore if necessary.

A tattoo is harder to disguise than a piercing, especially if it has been done in an obvious place. Sometimes people feel they cannot live with their tattoo any longer. Until recently there would have been very little they could do except to have the skin in which the tattoo was embedded cut out, leaving a terrible scar. Today it is possible to have a tattoo removed using lasers.

Someone who decides that they no longer want a tattoo should first go to see their doctor, who will be able to give advice on where to get the tattoo removed as safely as possible.

How tattoo removal works

Laser tattoo removal works by **vaporizing** the colours injected under the skin by the tattooist. Because certain colours only absorb some forms of light, different lasers have to be used to remove different colours. Black, which absorbs all forms of light, is the easiest tattoo colour to remove; green and yellow are the hardest. Removal of a complicated tattoo with lots of colours takes several visits.

Even though laser removal of a tattoo is less risky and painful than any other method, there are still risks. Most of these relate to what is left once the tattoo has been removed: sometimes the skin either loses all its colour or has too much colour. Either way, a strange blotch is left behind. The site of the tattoo can also become infected, and there is a 5 per cent chance that a permanent scar will be left behind.

Laser removal of a tattoo is an unrealistic option for most people because of the high cost. This means that nearly everyone who has a tattoo they no longer like is stuck with it.

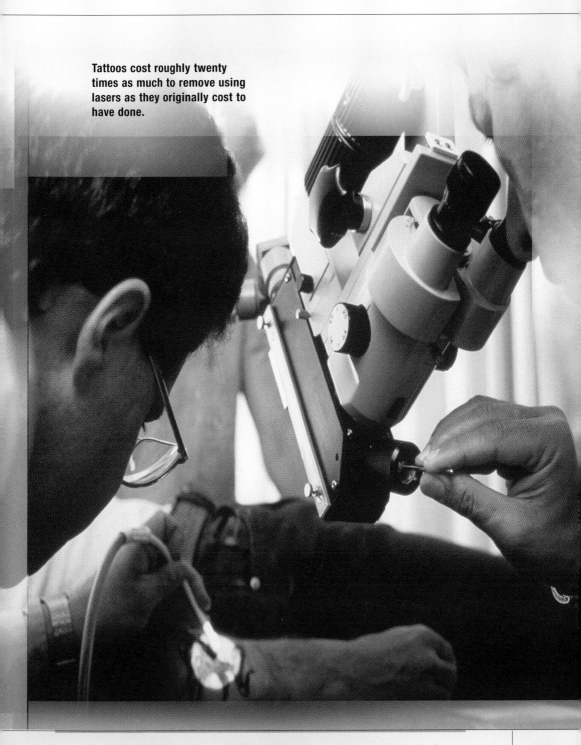

Tattoos cost roughly twenty times as much to remove using lasers as they originally cost to have done.

Legal matters

Most Western governments feel that young people should not be allowed to have tattoos before a certain age, and have made laws to stop them. Usually these laws say that young people should not be allowed to have a tattoo until they have become an adult – at age eighteen in many countries. Stricter laws on tattooing age limits have been encouraged by horrified parents whose children have had tattoos done. For example, the ban on tattooing under-eighteens in Arizona, USA was linked to a campaign by a mother whose fifteen-year-old daughter came home with a tattoo.

Laws on age limits for having a piercing are less common, but piercing can be dealt with as an assault on a **minor**. If a minor gets a piercing without the permission of their parent or guardian, the police could become involved. If the parent makes a complaint, the piercer could be charged with assault or **wounding**, and could end up in jail. Many piercing studios refuse to pierce people under the age of eighteen, partly because of the legal consequences and partly because there can be health problems with some piercings if they are done at a young age.

Health regulation

Regulations covering health and safety requirements vary from one country to another, and even within a country. In 1994, for example, 13 US states had regulations governing tattoo studios, 34 had no regulations, and 2 states banned tattooing altogether (Oklahoma and South Carolina). The final state, Florida, had a unique set of laws.

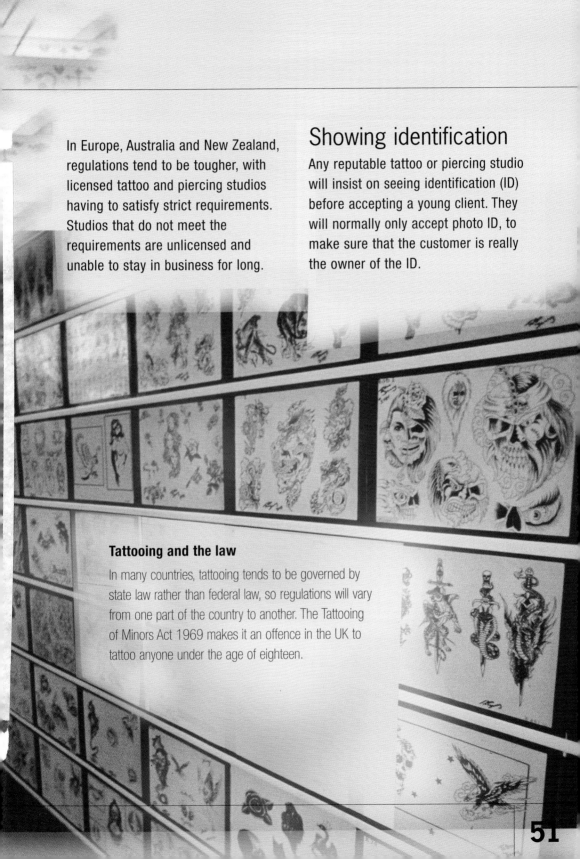

In Europe, Australia and New Zealand, regulations tend to be tougher, with licensed tattoo and piercing studios having to satisfy strict requirements. Studios that do not meet the requirements are unlicensed and unable to stay in business for long.

Showing identification

Any reputable tattoo or piercing studio will insist on seeing identification (ID) before accepting a young client. They will normally only accept photo ID, to make sure that the customer is really the owner of the ID.

Tattooing and the law

In many countries, tattooing tends to be governed by state law rather than federal law, so regulations will vary from one part of the country to another. The Tattooing of Minors Act 1969 makes it an offence in the UK to tattoo anyone under the age of eighteen.

Information and advice

The first port of call for most people who have a problem as a result of tattooing or body piercing is their doctor. Usually it is best to get advice as quickly as possible. A doctor may be able to provide literature for patients to take away and read, and will normally be able to find out where patients can go for **counselling** or tattoo removal advice.

Information about tattooing and body piercing is fairly limited. Readers tempted to find out more about these subjects may be able to find some information from local libraries, although some of the books that are published on the subject are either very old, or modern books on stars and their tattoos. There are also lots of books showing photos of tattoos and body piercings, but these rarely give very much useful information.

One of the best places for information about tattooing is the Internet. Information on body piercing is also available on the Internet, but it is harder to find informative or useful websites.

The websites listed here provide some useful information on tattooing and body piercing:

www.howstuffworks.com

An excellent entry on tattooing gives information on most aspects of the subject.

www.safetattoos.com and **www.safepiercing.org**

These are the home sites of the Alliance of Tattooing Professionals and the Association of Professional Piercers. Each of these is a non-profit organization dedicated to raising health and information standards in the tattooing and piercing industries.

www.smh.com.au/news

An article in this section from 30 May 2001 gives information on the numbers of Australians with tattoos and piercings, and the possibility of diseases spreading.

www.tattooarchive.com

This is a general site with a limited amount of information on subjects such as The Great Omi. The site also contains a variety of articles about the historical and cultural significance of tattooing.

Disclaimer
All the Internet addresses (URLs) given in this book were valid at the time of going to press. However, due to the dynamic nature of the Internet, some addresses may have changed, or sites may have changed or ceased to exist since publication. While the author and Publisher regret any inconvenience this may cause readers, no responsibility for any such changes can be accepted by either the author or the Publisher.

Further reading

None of the following books are specifically aimed at school-age readers, but all of them contain some information that could be useful or interesting:

Memoirs of a Tattooist, by George Burchett; London: Oldbourne, 1958
This fascinating book is the autobiography of 'Professor' George Burchett, who tattooed sailors, soldiers, society ladies and members of Europe's royal families, as well as American industrialists and South African businessmen. Although this book is now out of print, large libraries may still have a copy.

Celebrity Skin: Tattoos, Brands and Body Adornments of the Stars, by Jim Gerard; Hove: Apple, 2001
A trashy but very entertaining look at some of the tattoos sported by some of today's celebrities, including musicians, actors, models and athletes.

The Body Art Book: A Complete, Illustrated Guide to Tattoos, Piercings, and Other Body Modifications, by Jean-Chris Miller; Berkley: Berkley Publishing Group, 1997

Decorated Skin, by Karl Groning; London: Thames and Hudson, 2001
A collection of photographs of tattoos and piercings introduced by a brief essay on the subject.

Glossary

acne pitting
minor scars caused by the skin condition acne

allergy/allergic reaction
an unexpected and unpleasant physical reaction to something

anti-social
behaviour that goes against socially expected ways of behaving

autoclave
a high-temperature device that kills any germs inside it. Autoclaves are used by tattooists and piercers to sterilize their re-usable equipment.

back-street
a term used to describe something that is hidden, secretive and often illegal

chisel
a bar of metal or wood with one flat end and one sharp end: the flat end is hit with a hammer to drive the sharp end into or under something

counsellor
a professional person who listens to someone talk through a problem, without being judgemental

dermis
the inner layer of a human's skin

facial tattooing
tattooing of a person's face

freak show
a popular form of entertainment during the 19th century. Freak shows contained all sorts of unusual things – including oddly tattooed people or bearded ladies. Today they are considered cruel as they 'cashed in' on people's misfortunes.

glacier
a thick sheet of ice that flows out of a snow-bound valley

gladiators
Roman slaves who were paid to fight dangerous animals or fierce warriors to entertain crowds of people

Hell's Angels
members of gangs of motorcyclists, famous for their lawless behaviour

hepatitis B, hepatitis C
a virus that can be passed from one person to another by infected blood and blood-stained body fluids and by having sex with an infected person. The infection can cause long-term liver damage.

HIV
Human Immunodeficiency Virus. HIV attacks and destroys the body's immune system.

hygiene/hygienic
cleanliness and being free from germs

lubricant
an agent – a gel or a cream, for example – that is used to reduce friction between two objects that rub together

Maori
the first humans to live in New Zealand, and their descendants

minor
people, for example children, who are not legally responsible for themselves are known as minors

mummified
preserved after death through drying out

Olympic rings
the five inter-linked rings that make up the symbol of the Olympic Games

organic
grown without the use of artificial fertilizers or other chemicals

pain threshold
the level of pain a person can withstand

permanent
non-removable

piercing gun
a mechanical device that is sometimes used to perform piercings. Most professional piercers say that hand-held needles are more hygienic than piercing guns, because they are thrown away after a single use and so cannot pass on diseases to other people.

Polynesian
the term used to describe something or someone that comes from Polynesia – an area in the Pacific Ocean

regulated
governed by a set of rules and regulations, usually those made and enforced by the government or the state

Roman legions
the name for the units into which the armies of Ancient Rome were organized

shrapnel
pieces of metal created when a bomb or shell explodes. The bomb or shell case breaks apart; the pieces are known as shrapnel.

smallpox
a highly infectious disease that killed many people until the 20th century. Those who survived smallpox were often left with scarring on their face and elsewhere.

specialist
in the medical world, a specialist is someone who is an expert in a particular kind of subject

stencil
the outline of a shape, which can either be filled in to make a finished picture or left as an outline

sterilized
cleaned, so that any germs or viruses are killed and cannot spread further infection, for example equipment that is used in the piercing or tattooing process must be sterile

surgery
a medical procedure that involves a doctor or surgeon cutting the skin of a patient

symbolic
when one thing stands for another it is said to be a symbol or symbolic, for example, a country's flag can be a symbol for the nation

temporary
not permanent

unhygienic
not clean

vaporizing
turning to vapour; going from solid or liquid form to being a gas

wound
a cut or hole in the flesh

Index

Titles in the *Need to Know* series include:

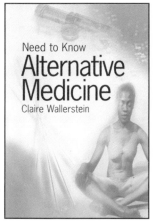

Need to Know
Alternative Medicine
Claire Wallerstein

Hardback   0 431 09808 5

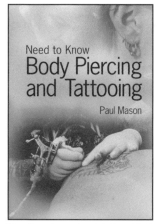

Need to Know
Body Piercing and Tattooing
Paul Mason

Hardback   0 431 09818 2

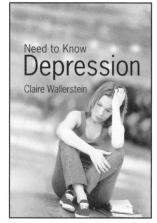

Need to Know
Depression
Claire Wallerstein

Hardback   0 431 09809 3

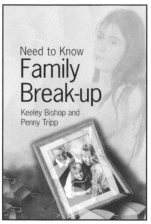

Need to Know
Family Break-up
Keeley Bishop and Penny Tripp

Hardback   0 431 09810 7

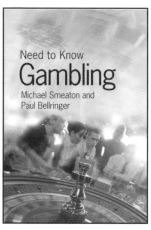

Need to Know
Gambling
Michael Smeaton and Paul Bellringer

Hardback   0 431 09819 0

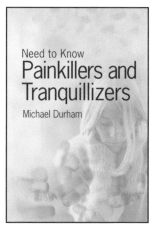

Need to Know
Painkillers and Tranquillizers
Michael Durham

Hardback   0 431 09811 5

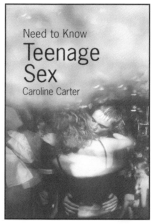

Need to Know
Teenage Sex
Caroline Carter

Hardback   0 431 09821 2

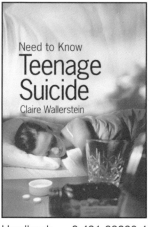

Need to Know
Teenage Suicide
Claire Wallerstein

Hardback   0 431 09820 4

Find out about the other titles in this series on our website www.heinemann.co.uk/library